W9-CDN-637

Jimi

Sounds Like a Rainbow

A Story of the Young Jimi Hendrix

by Gary Golio illustrated by Javaka Steptoe

Clarion Books
Houghton Mifflin Harcourt
Boston • New York
2010

Clarion Books ✷ 215 Park Avenue South, New York, New York 10003 ✷ The illustrations were executed in mixed media. ✷ The text was set in Trade Gothic Bold. ✷ Clarion Books is an imprint of Houghton Mifflin Harcourt Publishing Company ✷ www.hmhbooks.com ✷ Manufactured in China ✷ Library of Congress Cataloging-in-Publication Data ✷ Golio, Gary. ✷ Jimi : sounds like a rainbow : a story of the young Jimi Hendrix / by Gary Golio ; illustrated by Javaka Steptoe. ✷ p. cm. ✷ Includes bibliography, discography, videography, and web resources. ✷ ISBN 978-0-618-85279-6 ✷ 1. Hendrix, Jimi—Juvenile literature. 2. Rock musicians—United States—Biography—Juvenile literature. I. Steptoe, Javaka,1971–, ill. II. Title.
ML3930.H45G65 2010 ✷ 787.87'166092—dc22
[B] ✷ 2009047727
LEO 10 9 8 7 6 5 4 3 2 1
4500218503

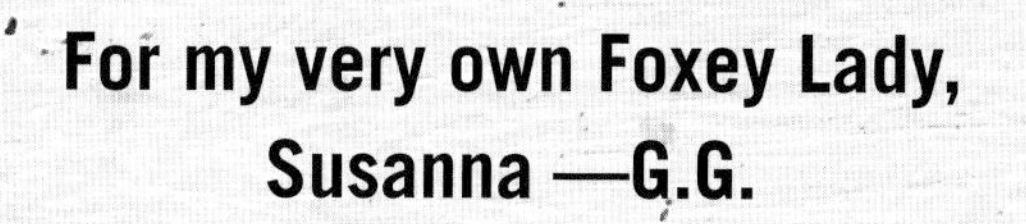

For my very own Foxey Lady,
Susanna —G.G.

To my mother, Stephanie Douglas,
my father, John Steptoe, and little
Marion Walter Jacobs —J.S.

"Music is magic." —Jimi Hendrix

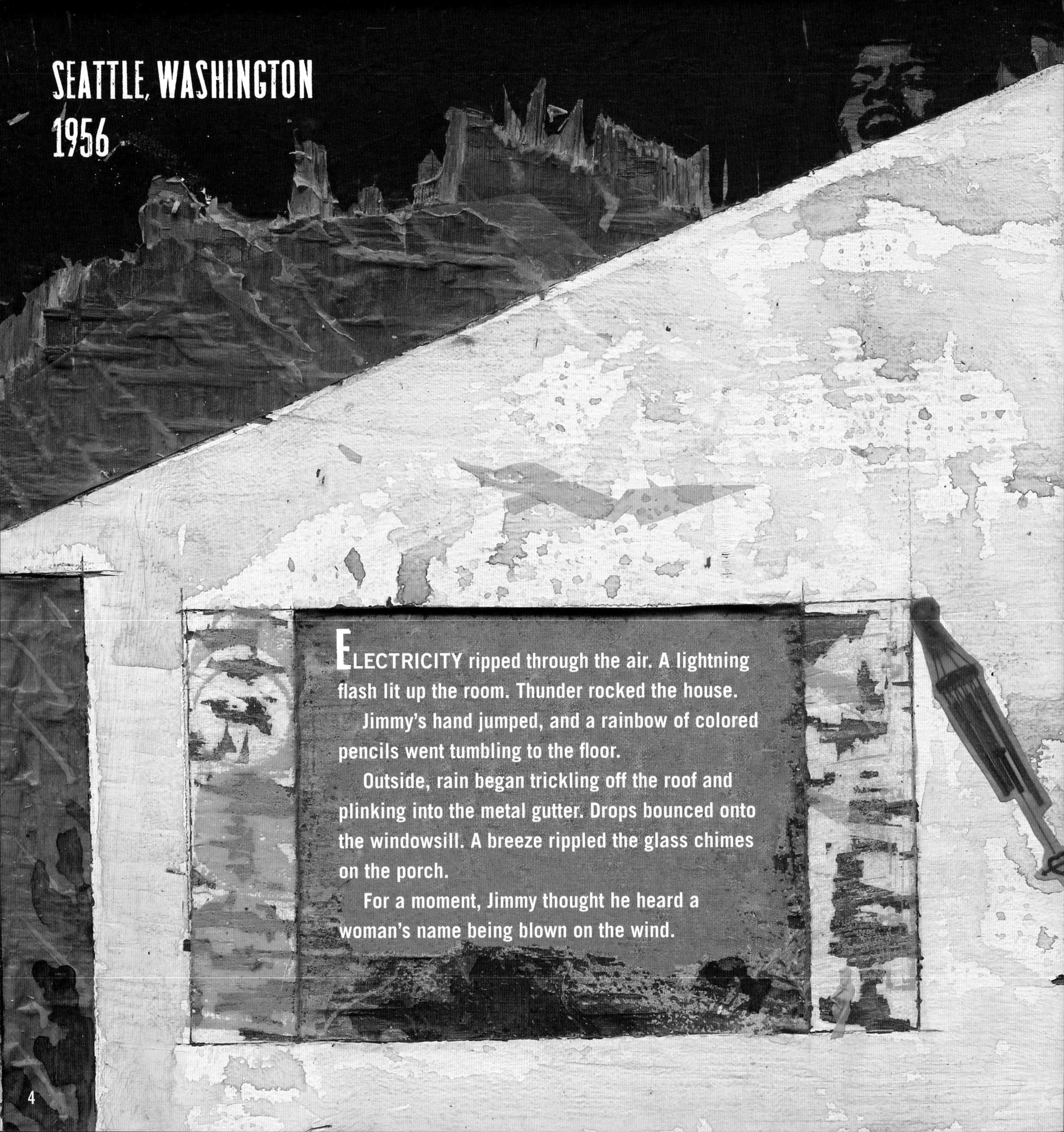

SEATTLE, WASHINGTON 1956

ELECTRICITY ripped through the air. A lightning flash lit up the room. Thunder rocked the house.

Jimmy's hand jumped, and a rainbow of colored pencils went tumbling to the floor.

Outside, rain began trickling off the roof and plinking into the metal gutter. Drops bounced onto the windowsill. A breeze rippled the glass chimes on the porch.

For a moment, Jimmy thought he heard a woman's name being blown on the wind.

Jimmy grabbed his one-string ukulele. He could play only simple tunes, but now he had a new idea.

He pulled the string and let it snap back, tapping gently with his finger, up and down the neck, to get just the right notes.

Over and over.

Until he could play the sound of raindrops,

singing as they fell.

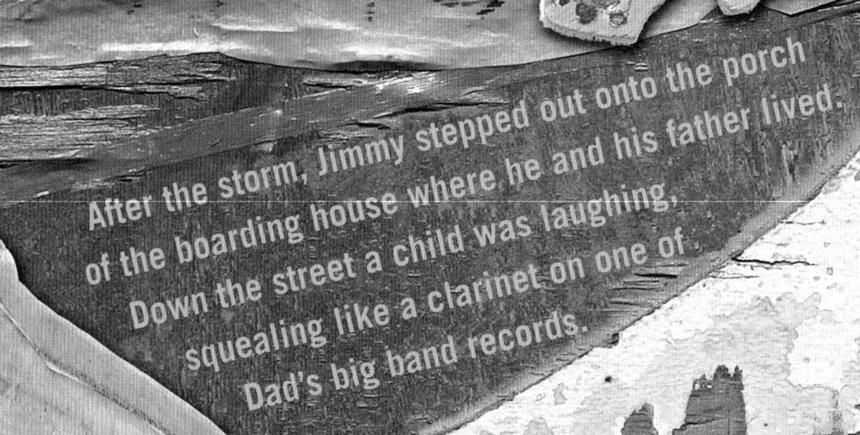

After the storm, Jimmy stepped out onto the porch of the boarding house where he and his father lived. Down the street a child was laughing, squealing like a clarinet on one of Dad's big band records.

A truck engine backfired, pounding like a bass drum, as a neighbor's rake played snare against the sidewalk. A dog yowled, a siren wailed in the distance, and a bird rattled off a string of high, wild notes.

The sounds of life were calling out, and Jimmy Hendrix wanted to answer them.

Terry and Potato Chip waved from across the street. They loved Jimmy's drawings, the funny stories he told, the way he could imitate guitars and trumpets with his mouth and hands.

And they never teased him about his worn-out clothes and wild hair, the way some kids did. Or because he was always moving from one part of town to another when Dad was out of work. They were the Three Musketeers, best friends for life!

Down at the record store, the boys checked out the Top 10 hits each week. Crazy about music, they would chatter for hours about the latest rock 'n' roll songs. Elvis Presley, Chuck Berry, and B.B. King—the airwaves were sizzling with exciting new sounds and rhythms.

SHOP
"CLOSE TO THE CORNER
SITUATION THE SQUARE"
SWING • JAZZ • POPULAR
CLASSICAL • ALL LEADING
NAME BANDS • SINGERS
DRExel 8482
ME HEAR
OF THAT
'N' ROLL

Sometimes, Jimmy and his friends bicycled down to the lake, a magical place of deep green leaves and dark purple shadows. They'd throw rocks in the water, listening to them plop and gurgle as they sank.

All around, there were birds singing, bees buzzing, and breezes whistling through trees. Above the clouds, airplane engines droned and whirred.

With every sound, a color glowed in Jimmy's mind.

Blue was the whoosh of cool water, splashing over rocks.

Orange and red, the crackling of a campfire.

Green, the rustle of a thousand leaves.

At home, Jimmy drew and painted for hours. He filled pages with sleek-finned spaceships, knights on horseback, fierce Indian chiefs, and castles in the clouds. A teacher even let him cover the blackboards once with chalk drawings of Mexico—in bold, blazing yellows, purples, and reds.

Jimmy's imagination was on fire, and a tune was always playing in his head.

At night, he'd listen to Dad croon along with gospel, jazz, or blues records on the old phonograph. A song by Muddy Waters—with its wailing guitar and harmonica—set off fireworks in his mind.

He wondered: Could a person use music like chalks and colored pencils?

Could someone paint pictures with sound?

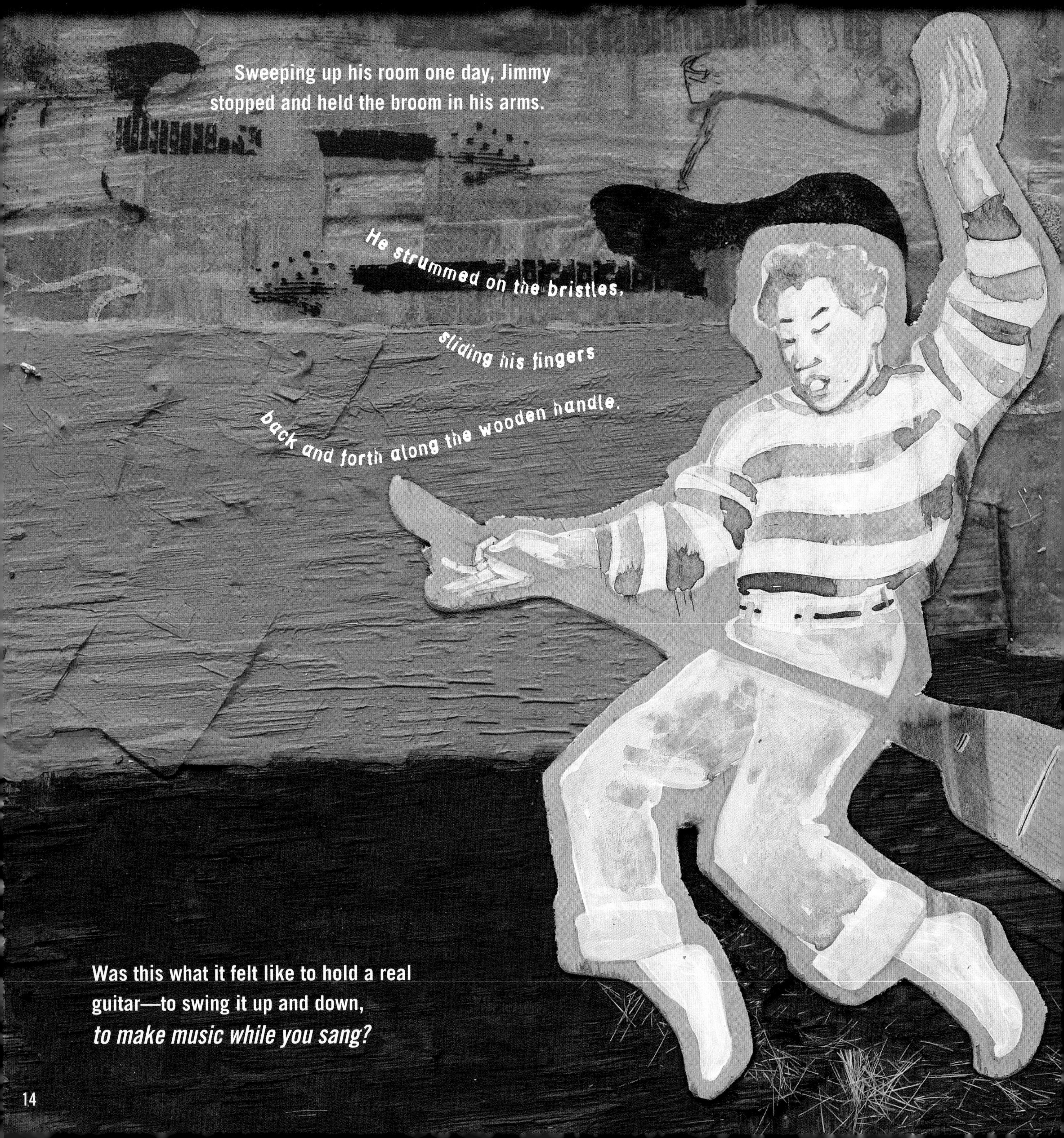

Sweeping up his room one day, Jimmy stopped and held the broom in his arms.

He strummed on the bristles,

sliding his fingers

back and forth along the wooden handle.

Was this what it felt like to hold a real guitar—to swing it up and down, *to make music while you sang?*

On the radio, Elvis Presley's hit "Hound Dog" shook the speaker. Elvis was the King, twisting and shouting to the beat of rock 'n' roll.

Jimmy strummed the broom again. Pieces of straw went flying into the air as he wiggled his hips like Elvis and sang his heart out for an imaginary audience of screaming fans.

Sitting on the porch one night, Jimmy watched as the landlady's son cradled a worn wooden guitar in his lap and began to sing. The man's voice was dark and smooth, like velvet.

The blues, they is a lonely sound,
Like the whistle of a train,
Full of tender feelings,
And pourin' down like rain . . .

Notes spun from the strings,
flickering in the air
like fireflies.

Jimmy's eyes shone. He could feel the music tingling in his fingertips.

When the landlady's son offered to sell his guitar for five dollars, Jimmy begged Dad to buy it.

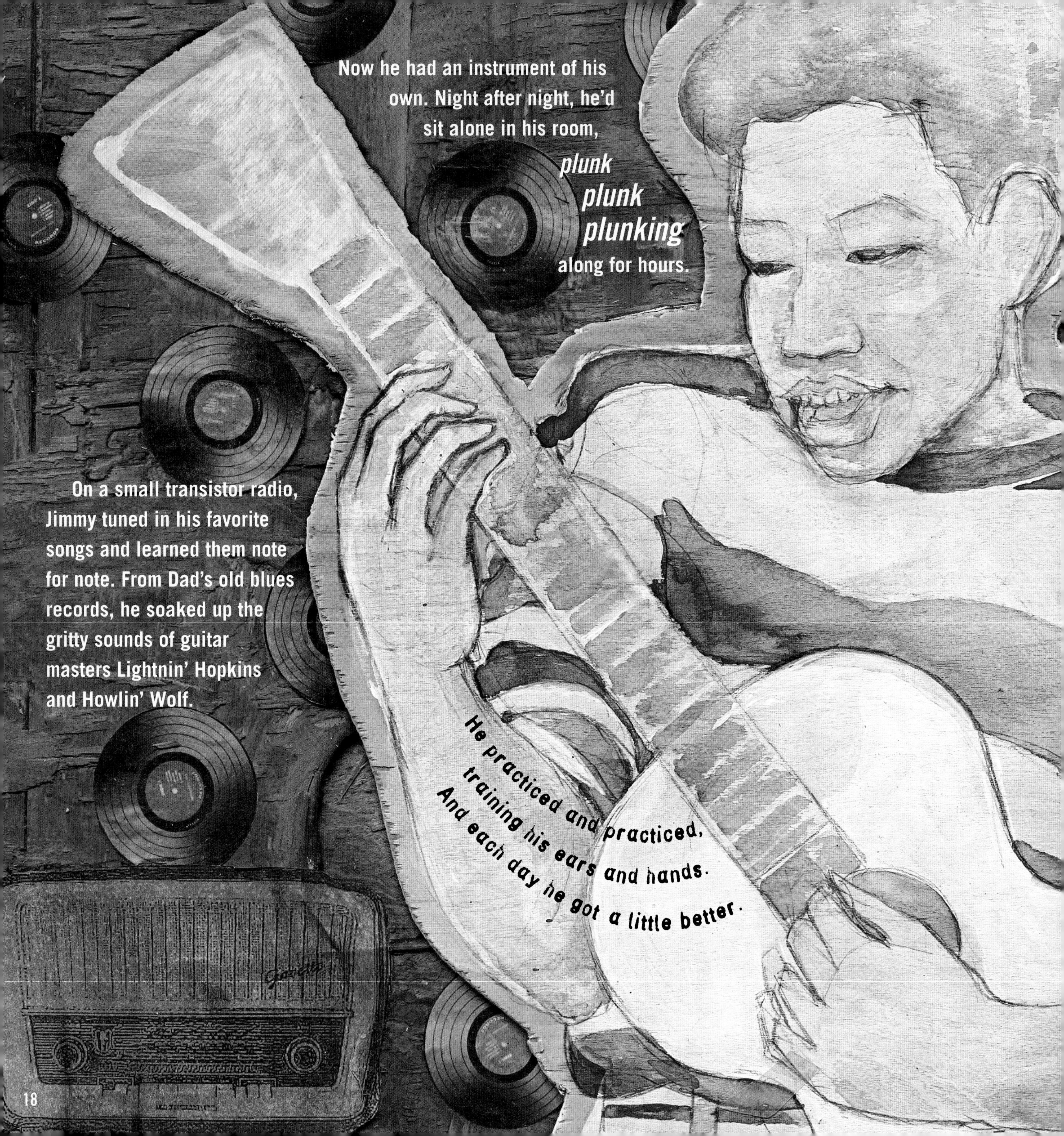

Now he had an instrument of his own. Night after night, he'd sit alone in his room,

plunk

plunk

plunking

along for hours.

On a small transistor radio, Jimmy tuned in his favorite songs and learned them note for note. From Dad's old blues records, he soaked up the gritty sounds of guitar masters Lightnin' Hopkins and Howlin' Wolf.

He practiced and practiced, training his ears and hands. And each day he got a little better.

Before long, Jimmy could play the guitar while Potato Chip sang, or jam with Terry as his fingers tickled the keys of an old piano in the basement.

Every note, and every chord, was like a new color for Jimmy.

He had a rainbow of sounds at his fingertips, and he wanted to paint the world with them.

Soon, Jimmy played well enough to join a local band. But when he first performed onstage, the screaming saxophone, pounding drums, and rocking piano drowned out his old wooden guitar. He felt invisible.

If he wanted to be heard, he'd need a louder guitar—an *electric* guitar. Money was tight, but Dad could see what music meant to his son.

It may have been the cheapest model, but to Jimmy, his new white Supro Ozark guitar was pure gold.

Now he could plug into an amplifier, turn up the volume, and hold his own in the band.

With the flick of a switch, Jimmy's life was electrified!

Practicing at a friend's house one day, Jimmy heard the amplifier making strange and eerie sounds. Out of the speaker came buzzes and whistles, fuzzy hissing, and a raspy humming. Strumming the guitar made the noises shift and change.

By turning knobs and stretching guitar strings, Jimmy found that he could play with the different sounds. He ran his fingers up and down the neck, tapping and scraping, plucking, sliding, and picking. Then a smile flashed across his face.

Suddenly, the room filled with a rocket's roar. Crashing waves. The buzz of swarming bees. Jimmy was finally painting with sound!

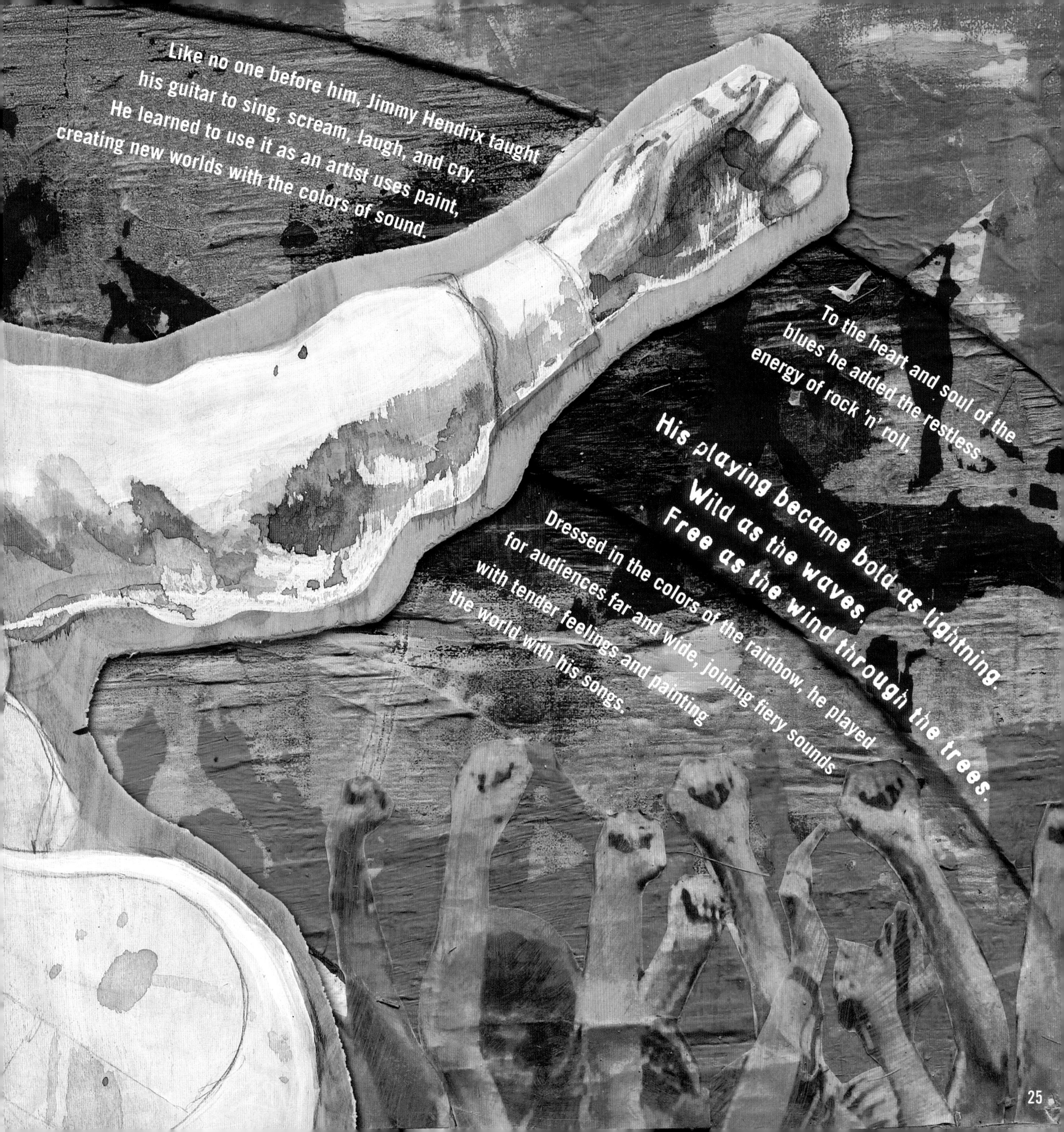

Like no one before him, Jimmy Hendrix taught his guitar to sing, scream, laugh, and cry. He learned to use it as an artist uses paint, creating new worlds with the colors of sound.

To the heart and soul of the blues he added the restless energy of rock 'n' roll.

His playing became bold as lightning. Wild as the waves. Free as the wind through the trees.

Dressed in the colors of the rainbow, he played for audiences far and wide, joining fiery sounds with tender feelings and painting the world with his songs.

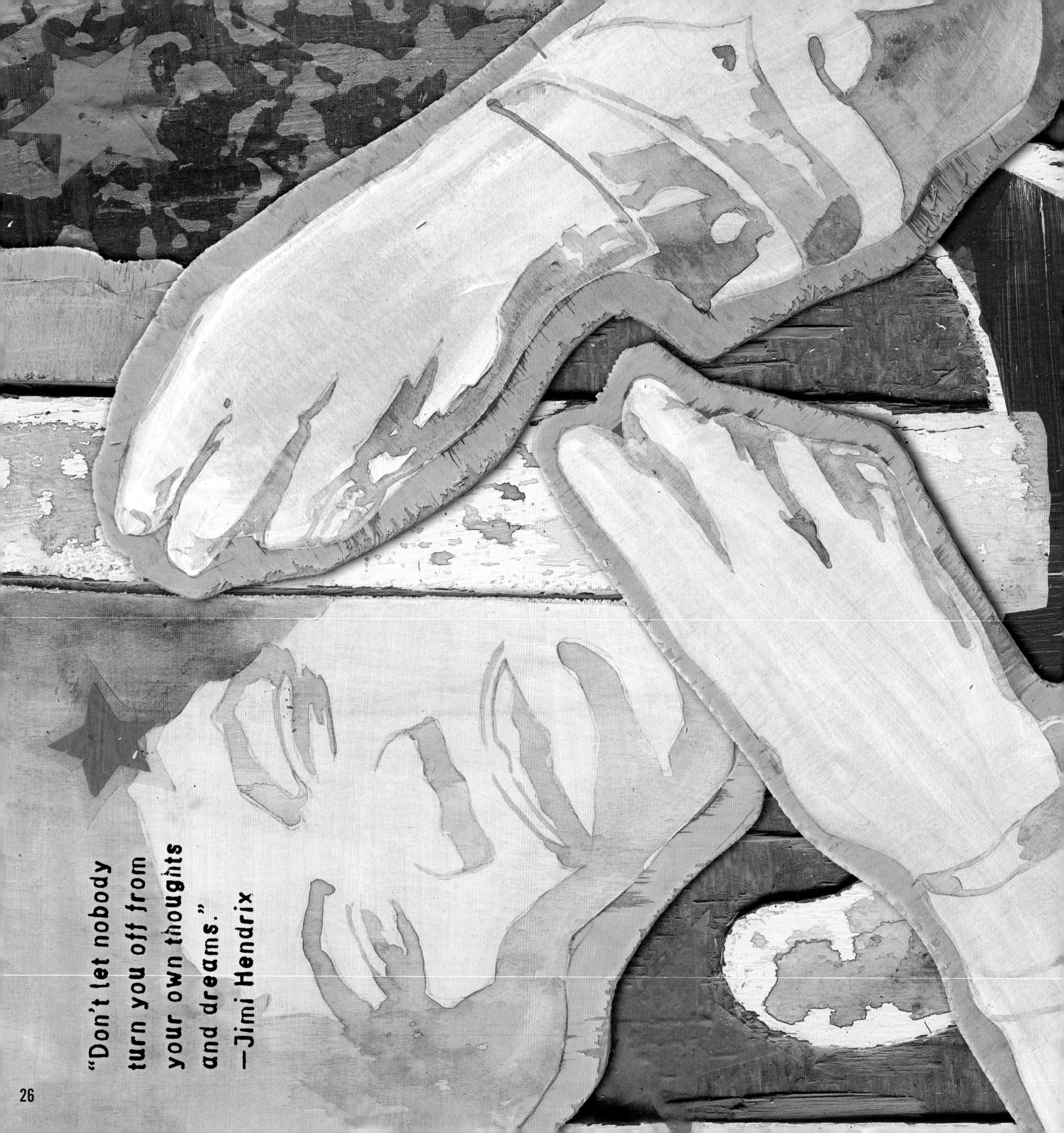

"Don't let nobody
turn you off from
your own thoughts
and dreams."
—Jimi Hendrix

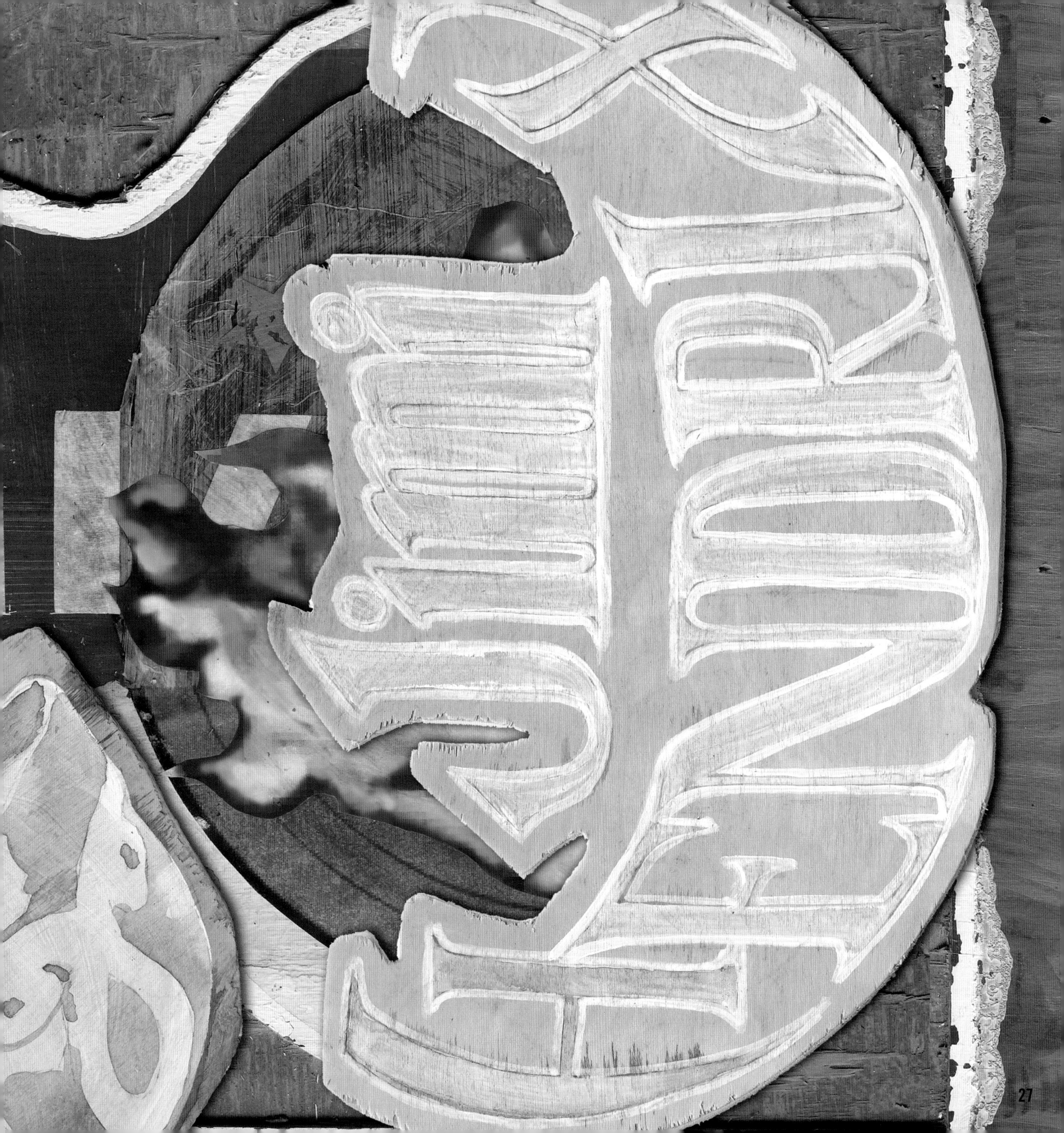

MORE ABOUT JIMI HENDRIX

BORN in 1942, James Marshall Hendrix grew up in Seattle, Washington—the perfect place for a boy whose veins flowed with the blood of Cherokee Indians, African slaves, and white Europeans. People of all colors lived in the "Rainbow City" then, and Jimmy learned lessons of tolerance there that lent a universal quality to his music later on.

At eighteen, Jimmy joined the Army's 101st Airborne Division and became a paratrooper. After his discharge, he toured the country from 1962 to 1966 as a backup guitarist, working with top Motown and rhythm and blues performers like Little Richard, Sam Cooke, and the Isley Brothers. He even met two of his musical heroes, Muddy Waters and B.B. King.

In the fall of 1966, music manager Chas Chandler took Jimmy to England. There, he changed the spelling of his name and formed the Jimi Hendrix Experience. Touring Europe with his new band, Jimi created a sensation. His thrilling stage moves and explosive guitar playing led reporters to name him the "Wild Man of Borneo" and the "Black Elvis." The racial makeup of the Experience was also unique at that time: a three-person band with a white drummer and white bass player, led by a black guitarist. When the band made their American debut at the Monterey Pop Festival in 1967, Jimi set fire to his guitar onstage and became a legend overnight.

With tools like the wah-wah pedal and fuzz box, and revolutionary recording techniques developed in the studio, Jimi created a new language of sound for the guitar. His first three albums—*Are You Experienced?, Axis: Bold as Love,* and *Electric*

Ladyland—are rock 'n' roll classics, and Jimi is still considered the greatest electric guitarist of all time by music fans worldwide.

Jimi's music is so unusual because he soaked up everything around him and made it his own. At a time when music, like society, was still largely divided by race, he blended styles and sounds without regard to color. He listened to folksingers like Bob Dylan, Indian musicians like Ravi Shankar, and jazz masters like Miles Davis, and to the classical works of Bach and Handel. The advice of his father, Al, always rang true: "Be original. Do your own thing."

Jimi believed that music was a powerful healing force, and he spoke often about the concept of "Electric Church"—his own use of song and sound to spiritually uplift and transform an audience. He also supported Martin Luther King Jr. and the civil rights movement of the 1960s, and hoped that his music would bring about positive social change. His electrifying version of "The Star-Spangled Banner," performed at the Woodstock Music Festival in 1969, was a passionate personal statement about the violence and tragedy of war.

Jimi died in 1970. Yet to this day, his music touches people of all ages, all over the world. He is considered a great example of what a true artist can be—someone with new ideas who respects creativity in all its forms. Pop, rock, country, hip-hop, classical, and jazz musicians all admire and learn from his work. He did things with the guitar that no one before him had dreamed of doing, and he encouraged us to keep on dreaming.

"When I die, just keep playing the records." —Jimi Hendrix

AUTHOR'S NOTE

JIMI Hendrix died at the age of twenty-seven from an unfortunate combination of prescription drugs and alcohol. Some unfamiliar sleeping pills—taken after an exhausting series of concerts and interviews—slowed down his breathing, and he suffocated during the night on food and drink from his dinner. Those close to Jimi knew how much he loved life, and doctors ruled his death an accident.

Still, Jimi's substance use plays a large part in how he is remembered today. Like many other musicians—and many young people during the 1960s—he experimented with drugs like LSD and marijuana, believing that they could "open your mind," "expand your consciousness," and maybe even help to make you more creative as an artist or musician.

Perhaps the greatest tragedy of Jimi's untimely death is that we will never know just what he might have accomplished had his difficulties with alcohol and drugs been addressed and treated. As a clinical social worker who has worked with hundreds of teens and adults suffering from addiction problems, I have seen how alcoholism and substance use often follow physical or emotional abuse, depression, childhood poverty, and the loss of one's parents at an early age. The death of Jimi's mother when he was fifteen—years after she had left the family—made for feelings of emptiness and sadness that stayed with him all his life.

In the spirit of recognizing that addiction is a treatable disease, and that deaths like Jimi's can be prevented, here are some resources for better understanding and addressing the dangers of substance use.

WEBSITES

Building Blocks for a Healthy Future [ages 3–6]
An early childhood prevention program developed by the Substance Abuse and Mental Health Services Administration (SAMHSA, U.S. Department of Health and Human Services) to educate parents, caregivers, and children about the basics. *bblocks.samhsa.gov*

Reach Out Now Teach-In [ages 10–11]
A public education initiative that provides communities with lesson plans and resources to educate middle-graders about the risks of underage alcohol use. *teachin.samhsa.gov*

WEBSITES [CONT.]

The Cool Spot [young teens]
Sponsored by SAMHSA and the National Institute on Alcohol Abuse and Alcoholism. This site's banner reads, "The young teen's place for info on alcohol and resisting peer pressure." With anime figures and fun quizzes. *thecoolspot.gov*

BOOKS

Faber, Adele, and Elaine Mazlish. *How to Talk So Kids Will Listen & Listen So Kids Will Talk.* New York: Avon Books, 1999.

Hong, K. L. *Life Freaks Me Out: And Then I Deal With It.* Minneapolis: Search Institute, 2005.

Newman, Susan. *It Won't Happen to Me: True Stories of Teen Alcohol and Drug Abuse.* New York: Perigee Books, 1987.

ILLUSTRATOR'S NOTE

Exploring the Inspiration Behind the Music

WHEN you are learning about a person and you really want to know about him, you can't just pick up a book. Even a good book won't tell you everything. To really know about a person, you have to do things that they did, and see the things they saw. So I listened to the music and watched performances on YouTube, I walked the streets of Jimi's hometown, Seattle, I read and thought about Jimi and talked to people who knew him, and I even fingered an electric guitar once or twice. In that green and lush city of magic, I listened for Jimi and asked for his help as I explored. I thought about guitars—their sound, their vibrations, their look and feel—so I used plywood I found at The RE Store in Ballard, a Seattle neighborhood. I thought about how Jimi saw the world and how that differed from other people's views, so I painted Jimi one way and his surroundings another way. I thought about the depth and texture of his music, so I layered and used bright colors: red, orange, yellow, green, blue, purple—rainbow colors. I visited Leschi Elementary, the school he attended, sat by the lake and saw Mount Washington, and visited Jimi's old home on Yesler Way, which gave me a tingling feeling as I approached.

This book is about the creative process of an artist. This is something that I can appreciate, being a creative person. No matter who we are creatively, we all basically follow the same path, but make the process our own and unique to us. (I explore such issues in a residency program called Exploring the Creative Process with Javaka Steptoe.) Creating the art for this book helped me to expand and grow and have a greater appreciation for music, Jimi's music, and the blues. All I can say is, Jimi rocks!

SOURCES AND RESOURCES

BOOKS

Henderson, David. *'Scuse Me While I Kiss the Sky: The Life of Jimi Hendrix.* New York: Bantam Books, 1981.

Hendrix, James A. *My Son Jimi.* As told to Jas Obrecht. Seattle: AlJas Enterprises, 1999.

Hendrix, Jimi. *Cherokee Mist: The Lost Writings.* Edited by Bill Nitopi. New York: HarperCollins, 1993.

Mitchell, Mitch, with John Platt. *Jimi Hendrix: Inside the Experience.* New York: St. Martin's Press, 1994.

Murray, Charles Shaar. *Crosstown Traffic: Jimi Hendrix and the Post-War Rock 'n' Roll Revolution.* New York: St. Martin's Press, 1991.

Shapiro, Harry, and Caesar Glebbeek. *Jimi Hendrix, Electric Gypsy.* New York: St. Martin's Press, 1991.

Willix, Mary. *Jimi Hendrix: Voices from Home.* San Diego: Creative Forces Publishing, 1995.

SELECTED DISCOGRAPHY: CDS, VIDEOS, AND DVDS

Hendrix, Jimi. *Blues.* Universal City, Calif.: MCA Records, 1994. CD.

———. *Valleys of Neptune.* New York. Sony Legacy Recordings, 2010. CD.

The Jimi Hendrix Experience. *Are You Experienced?* Universal City, Calif.: Experience Hendrix, LLC/MCA Records, distributed by Universal Music & Video Distribution, 1997. CD.

———. *Axis: Bold as Love.* Universal City, Calif.: MCA Records, 1993. CD.

———. *Electric Ladyland.* Universal City, Calif.: Experience Hendrix, LLC/MCA Records, distributed by Universal Music & Video Distribution, 1997. CD.

Jimi: Live at Woodstock. Santa Monica, Calif.: Experience Hendrix, LLC, 2005. DVD.

Jimi Hendrix: Live at Monterey. Seattle, Wash.: Experience Hendrix, LLC, 2007. DVD.

Wild Blue Angel: Jimi Hendrix at the Isle of Wight. Santa Monica, Calif.: MCA Records, 2002. DVD.

Woodstock: 3 Days of Peace & Music. Burbank, Calif.: Warner Home Video, 2009. DVD.

WEBSITES

jimihendrix.com The "official" Jimi Hendrix website, run by the Hendrix family–owned music company, Experience Hendrix, LLC.

emplive.com The website of Experience Music Project, an interactive music museum in Seattle.